Building a Better Youth Ministry

---

30 Ways in 30 Days

Trevor Hamaker

ISBN-10: 1532729898 ISBN-13: 978-1532729898

DOWNLOAD YOUR FREE GIFT

To say thank you for your purchase, I'd like to send you a FREE bonus package. This includes a cheat sheet of the 30 big ideas covered in this book, along with an mp3 coaching lesson on leading volunteers and a 2-week message series you can use with your students.

Download your FREE bonus package today at:

www.betteryouthministry.com/30days

SCAN

Contents

INTRODUCTION:

You're One Month Away...

I was at my son's soccer practice when my phone buzzed in my pocket. It was a number that I didn't recognize. Usually I let those calls go to my voicemail, but for some reason I answered it.

"Hello?"

The voice on the other end sounded like a young guy. Was it a college student? Maybe it was a former student of mine.

It was neither.

"Hi, is this Trevor?"

"Yes. Who is this?"

"You don't know me. My name is Brandon. Do you have a few minutes?"

Over the next 30 minutes, Brandon explained that he was concerned about his ministry. It was headed in the wrong direction.

Students weren't showing up.

Volunteers weren't engaged.

He was losing hope.

"Why isn't this working," he asked.

He'd been to seminary, but seminary hadn't prepared him for this.

"Can you help me do ministry better?" I

told him that I would be glad to help him.

We started meeting together.

We evaluated.

We dreamed.

We planned.

He got to work, and things started to turn around.

Students started showing up.

Volunteers started to care.

He regained his passion.

This book was written for youth pastors like Brandon.

What's My Experience?

I've worked as a youth pastor at 3 different churches:

1. A new church plant that met in a school.
2. A small, traditional church that is over 100 years old.
3. A large, contemporary church that is a strategic partner of North Point Ministries.

Each situation had different opportunities and challenges, but every one of them tripled in attendance under my leadership because I narrowed my focus to 5 things.

Five Things

If you will focus on these 5 things, your ministry will get better and grow bigger:

1. Place

The place where you meet must be appealing to students.

2. Preaching

The way you teach must be helpful for students.

3. Programs

The things you do must be engaging for students.

4. People

The volunteers you lead must be passionate about students.

5. Promotion

The way you get the word out must be relevant to students.

In this book, we will spend 5 days looking at each of these things. There could be entire books written about each one of them, but this book is designed to get you started in the right direction.

No matter what kind of church you're at, I believe that your ministry will get better and grow bigger when you get better in these 5 areas.

In their groundbreaking book, *Built to Last: Successful*

Habits of Visionary Companies, Jim Collins and Jerry Porras disclosed their findings from a six-year research project at the Stanford University School of Business. They had set out to learn what makes exceptional companies different from other companies.

Here's what they discovered:

Getting better is "a residual result of relentlessly asking the question, 'How can we improve ourselves to do better tomorrow than we did today?'"[1]

That's the guiding question for this book:

How can we improve ourselves to do better tomorrow than we did today?

What You'll Learn

In this book, we'll spend 30 days looking at 30 ways to take your ministry to the next level. This isn't fluff. Every one of these tips is packed with the potential to help you build a better youth ministry.

In the next 30 days, you'll learn how to:

Create goals that inspire peak performance.

Make small improvements that get big results. **Identify the areas that are holding your ministry back.**

Get access to resources that you thought were beyond your reach.

Keep students on the edge of their seats when you speak.

Plan a program that makes students say, "Wow!**"**

Inspire your volunteers to make a difference.

Make announcements that people remember.

Maximize your posts on social media.

Get first-time visitors to come back next week.

Ready to get started?

Now that you know where we're headed, let's get started...

PART 1:
Preparing the Way

*Getting Ready
to Move Forward*

DAY 1

Change Your Mind

Carol Dweck is a psychology professor at Stanford University. She's one of the world's leading researchers in the field of motivation. In her book, *Mindset: The New Psychology of Success,* she draws a contrast between the fixed mindset and the growth mindset.

She says that people with *fixed mindsets* see their potential as set in stone. They would say, "You are who you are, and that's who you'll always be. There's nothing you can do about it. You just have to live with it." These people don't believe that lasting change is possible, and they're quick to give up when obstacles get in their way.

On the other hand, she says the "*growth mindset* is based on the belief that your basic qualities are things you can cultivate through your efforts... The passion for stretching yourself and sticking to it, even (or especially) when it's not going well, is the hallmark of the growth mindset."[2]

Many of the youth pastors I coach have a fixed mindset

when it comes to their abilities. Not only that, they also have a fixed mindset when it comes to their church and their ministry.

They say things like, "This place is never going to change." Or, "Those people are set in their ways." Or, "Our group is never going to grow. We've tried everything." Maybe you've said those things yourself.

But what would happen if you adopted a growth mindset?

How might your thoughts about your abilities, your church, and your ministry be different if you approached them with the belief that they can change and get better?

Instead of saying, "Our group is never going to grow," you would say, "Our group hasn't grown yet, but we're on the brink of something big!"

What about dealing with those people who seem set in their ways?

Instead of seeing them as immovable obstacles, you could say, "They haven't come around yet, but I think we're making good progress." Do you see the difference?

As we start this journey together, it's important for you to understand that your mindset makes all the difference.

If you think it's **impossible**, it will be.

If you think it's **possible**, it is.

Today, your job is to change your mind.

DAY 2

Find a Partner

I worked as a personal trainer when I was in college. People would come to the gym and ask for my help. Some of them wanted to burn fat. Others wanted to build muscle.

I would walk them through the facility, show them how to use the equipment, and create workout plans for them.

These people had the best intentions; they really wanted to get results. But almost half of them didn't stick with the program for longer than two weeks.

Why did they give up?

They got busy.

They got distracted.

They felt like it was too much to do.

They fell back into familiar patterns.

That's what happened to nearly half of the people.

But the other half kept coming. They worked the plan. Eventually, they burned the fat. Eventually, they built the muscle. They're the ones who achieved their goals. Why did some people stick with it, while others didn't?

I was young, so I went to my manager to ask him that question. He pointed out something that I've never forgotten.

He said, "I've been in this business for a long time. Here's what I've seen: the people who have a workout partner – a friend at the gym or someone else they feel accountable to – follow through on their commitment. They show up and get the job done. They get the results they're looking for. The people who try to do it on their own just don't have enough willpower by themselves to get through it. They give up. **Everyone is better with a partner.**"

As I thought about what he said, I was convinced that he was right: *Everyone is better with a partner* The reason is simple:

A partner provides you with the accountability, support, encouragement, and motivation that are necessary to follow through on your commitments.

This commitment is no different. **If you're going to build a better youth ministry, you need to find a partner.**

You need to find someone who will hold you accountable, offer support, give encouragement, and add motivation. Ideally, it will be another youth pastor who will go through this book with you.

Proverbs 27:17 says, "As iron sharpens iron, so a friend sharpens a friend." That verse isn't just reserved for men's ministry t-shirts; its application is much broader than that.

Last week, my wife was cutting tomatoes in our kitchen. The knife wasn't making clean slices. It needed to be sharpened. She pulled out the sharpening rod and slid it down the edges of the knife a few times. That was all it took to get the knife cutting smoothly again.

That's the point of the proverb. We're better together. A partner helps you stay sharp so you can do the job that God has called you to do.

Today, your job is to find a partner.

DAY 3

Start Small

There's a phrase that I want you to say to yourself today. Are you ready for it?

Here it is…

Incremental Improvement.

Go ahead. Say it. Out loud.

Incremental Improvement

That's the key to better youth ministry.

Most people don't like to hear that. People like the spectacular, the overnight success, the quick turnaround. That's what gets people's attention. That's what makes people take notice, isn't it?

You *can* get attention. That's not hard. If you walk into Walmart without a shirt on, you'll get attention. It's just not the kind of attention you want.

You *can* draw a crowd. You *can* get more students to show up for one event than you've ever had before.

With the right marketing, anything is possible. But that's not the point.

The real question is:

Can you get students to come back next week?

That changes the focus from drawing a crowd to building a ministry.

Of course, your committed students will be back. They always come back. You could have the worst program in town and they would still be there.

But they aren't the ones we're talking about. We're talking about the students in the middle, the students who have a choice. They're the ones who have other things to do besides being at your church.

How are you going to reach them?

How are you going to keep them?

Say it with me:

Incremental Improvement.

Have you heard of Dave Brailsford?

In 2010, he was hired as the new Performance Director for Team Sky (Great Britain's professional cycling team). When he took over, no British cyclist had ever won the Tour de France.

He immediately implemented a system that focused on making marginal gains, or small improvements over time. He says, "The whole principle came from the idea that if you broke down everything you could think of that goes into riding a bike, and then improved it by 1%, you will get a significant increase when you put them all together."[3]

In other words, he believed that if you could get better

in every area by just 1%, then over time you would see remarkably better results.

He dug into every aspect of cycling. He examined the air pressure in tires. He revamped the weight training and conditioning program. He found the best nutritional supplements.

But he didn't stop there. He knew that cyclists aren't at their best when they're sick, so he taught his team how to properly wash their hands to reduce the risk of germs. He knew that rest was important for muscle recovery and stamina, so he sought out the best pillows for his team. They took those pillows everywhere they went.

That seems a bit much, doesn't it?

But it paid off. After only 3 years, Sir Bradley Wiggins from Team Sky became the first British cyclist to win the Tour de France. That was 2012. Later that year, the team also won 70% of the gold medals at the Olympics.

The next year, Chris Foome, another Team Sky cyclist, won the Tour de France.

Dave Brailsford didn't turn the team around overnight, but he helped them focus on getting better, 1% at a time.

The turnaround started with an emphasis on incremental improvement. Eventually, all of those small improvements added up to make a big difference. The same thing can happen for your ministry. If you get 1% better everyday, you'll be 365% better in a year.

Today, your job is to start small.

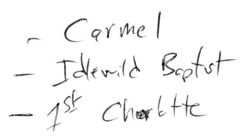

- Carmel
- Idlewild Baptist
- 1st Charlotte

DAY 4

Visit Another Church

It's easy to get stuck in a rut. You show up at the same place and do the same things every week. It can actually become comfortable.

A youth pastor once told me that as long as he showed up on time, ordered the Sunday School curriculum, booked the summer camp, and didn't teach heresy, everyone at his church would think he was doing a good job.

Do you think his ministry was growing or shrinking?

It was definitely shrinking. Attendance on Wednesday nights had dropped by 40% in two years.

As we talked, I could tell that his systems and programs were outdated. He hadn't stayed up to date with newer trends in youth ministry.

That happens to a lot of youth pastors. They get so wrapped up in what's going on at their own church, or in their own ministry, that they never break away to check out how things are being done elsewhere.

19

If you're stuck in a rut, going somewhere else to see how someone else does what you're trying to do can help you get unstuck.

In fact, I'd say that **visiting another church is one of the best ways to spark new ideas for your church.**

The one caution I would add is this:

Don't visit a church that is five times larger than your church.

Several years ago, I worked at a start-up church that met in a school and had 500 people in attendance on a Sunday morning. Our lead pastor took our team to a church that had 5,000 people in attendance on a Sunday morning.

We didn't leave inspired.

We left overwhelmed.

It was too much for us. At our scale, we were like a local high school marching band playing during halftime at a Friday night football game. The church we visited was like Bruno Mars playing during halftime at the Super Bowl. They were too far ahead of us for us to learn anything from them.

To make matters worse, on the ride home, our lead pastor said, "I don't see any reason why we can't do what they're doing." Some people call that vision. Our team called it delusional!

Instead of visiting the biggest church you can find, I recommend visiting a church that is two or three times larger than your church. What they're doing there will give you a lot more actionable ideas because they're closer to your size.

When you visit another church, don't show up unannounced. Send an email to the youth pastor a few days before. He'll appreciate the heads-up. Also, be sure to send a follow-up email thanking him for allowing you to come.

If your ministry schedule doesn't allow you to get away to observe another church's program in action, then reach out and ask if you can stop by to check out their student space and talk with the youth pastor about what they're doing and how they're doing it.

The insights I've gained from visiting other churches are worth more than a ticket to a 3-day youth ministry conference. And I've never had another youth pastor turn me down when I've asked to come. All you have to do is reach out and ask.

Today, your job is to find another church to visit.

DAY 5

Write a BHAG

A BHAG is a Big Hairy Audacious Goal. It's a super-sized version of the typical goals you might have.

Your typical goals are probably safe. When you go public with your goal to grow your ministry by 6 students in the next 12 months, no one really notices. But if you said, "My goal is to baptize 50 students in the next 24 months," then you would have their attention.

Jim Collins and Jerry Porras coined the term BHAG in their book, *Built to Last* They say, "A BHAG should not be a sure bet – perhaps only 50 to 70 percent probability of success – but the organization must believe 'we can do it anyway.' It should require extraordinary effort, and perhaps a little luck."[4]

In church, we call this a God-Sized Goal. It's the target you're aiming at that you can't accomplish in your own strength. You need God's help if it's going to happen.

In 1993, Dave Ramsey wrote down three BHAGs that he wanted to achieve within two years:

1. Broadcast his radio show in 25 cities.

2. Sell 50,000 copies of *Financial Peace.*

3. Teach Financial Peace University in 5 cities.

At that time, he'd recently self-published *Financial Peace,* his radio show was on one radio station, and he had taught Financial Peace University in 2 cities. Those goals seem pretty big, hairy, and audacious!

Fast forward to 1995. Here's what happened:

His radio show was in 12 cities.

He'd sold 100,000 copies of *Financial Peace* He'd taught Financial Peace University in 3 cities. Even though he hadn't reached his BHAGs, he was able achieve so much because he was aiming so high.

Today, Dave Ramsey's radio show is on the air in 480 cities, he has sold over 2 million copies of *Financial Peace,* and more than one million families have been through Financial Peace University.[5]

That's the power of a big hairy audacious goal.

Brian Tracy says, "Success is goals, and all else is commentary. All successful people are intensely goal oriented. They know what they want and they are focused single-mindedly on achieving it, every single day."[6]

Why don't we set big goals?

I think it comes down to a **fear of failure.** Small goals feel safe because they don't stretch you very far. If you simply show up and stay consistent, you'll more than likely reach your small goals. Big goals, on the other hand, push you to think differently and try new things.

Some of those things might not work out and you will need to adjust and try again.

Also, if you go public with a big goal, then you can be held accountable. People will know if you reached it or not.

When I worked at a church that was in steep decline, the pastor preached a sermon about the power of goals. I thought that was ironic because I was the only person on our staff that had publicly stated any ministry goals. When I asked him what his goals were, he couldn't give me an answer. I wish he'd been more willing to practice what he preached.

Meanwhile, I had told our church that it was my goal to double the number of students within 12 months.

I'll admit it. That was scary. I had put myself out there with that goal. Before I had arrived, the church had lost 50% of their students. Here I was saying that we were going to get them all back. It was a BHAG, for sure.

But it happened. After 12 months, we had doubled the number of students who attended our church. After 18 months, we had tripled that number. All the while, the attendance in other ministries at the church continued to decline.

When you write down a Big Hairy Audacious Goal, you're setting the priority for your ministry. You're deciding how you'll use your time, where you'll place your focus, and how you'll spend your money. It's a big decision, but it brings big results.

Today, your job is to write down a BHAG.

100^3

WEEK IN REVIEW

Day 1:

Adopt a growth mindset. If you think it's impossible, it will be. If you think it's possible, it is.

Day 2:

Find a partner to work with. A partner provides you with the accountability, support, encouragement, and motivation that are necessary to follow through on your commitments.

Day 3:

Make incremental improvements. The real question is: Can you get students to come back next week? That changes the focus from drawing a crowd to building a ministry.

Day 4:

Visit another church that is twice your size. The insights I've gained from visiting other churches are worth more than a ticket to a 3-day youth ministry conference.

Day 5:

Write a Big Hairy Audacious Goal. It's a super-sized version of the typical goals you might have. When you write down a Big Hairy Audacious Goal, you're setting the priority for your ministry.

PART 2:
Paying Attention to Your Place

Designing a Space That Appeals to Students

DAY 6

Evaluate Your Place

Students who visit your church usually decide whether or not they're going to come back before your program even starts.

Some people say the decision is made within the first seven minutes. Others say it's made within the first eleven minutes.[7] Either way, the data does suggest that students have made up their minds about coming back before any games have been played or songs been sung.

At that point, the decision isn't necessarily rational; it's reactionary. Nelson Searcy nails it when he says, "They're not weighing the pros and cons of your worship style and theological viewpoints. Instead, they are taking in clues about your church's atmosphere and people's friendliness on a much more rudimentary level."[8] The decision is being made beneath the surface, in the student's subconscious mind.

It's not based on your speaking ability, it's based on what

a student sees happening when they first show up at your place.

A student's experience at your church begins as their parents pull into the parking lot. Consider the following questions:

- Are there people in the parking lot to direct the flow of traffic and greet people as they arrive?
- Are there pot holes that need to be fixed?
- Is the landscaping kept up?
- Does the building look maintained and cared for?
- Is it easy to find the proper entrance?

Some churches have a separate building for students. That was the case at one of the churches I've worked at. The building was on an adjacent property to the church.

The first thing I noticed in my evaluation was that there weren't any signs to indicate that students met in that other building. In fact, there weren't any signs to indicate that the building even belonged to the church at all! It just looked like an old, abandoned building.

This is the time to make a note about that kind of thing.

When a student steps inside your student ministry environment, you want their first thought to be, "Wow!" That's what people say when you exceed their expectations. They say, "Wow!" when things are better, nicer, brighter, and cleaner than they thought they would be.

Mark Waltz, executive pastor at Granger Community Church in Indiana, says, "If our guests can't say, 'Wow!

I'm impressed!' within their first ten minutes on our campus, then we've failed."[9]

I think "failed" might be too strong of a word, but I like what he's aiming at.

As you evaluate your place, consider these questions to get you started:

- What's on the walls?
- Are any light bulbs out?
- Are there any old papers or trash lying around?
- Is there any broken stuff (ping pong tables, TVs, couches, chairs, etc.)?
- Are there any weird smells?
- Are the restrooms clean and stocked with toilet paper, soap, and paper towels?
- Does the audio/visual equipment work well?
- Are there typos or misspellings on printed materials or slides?
- Does it feel like somewhere a student would *want* to be?

You don't need to try to fix any of these today. That will come later.

Today, your job is only to evaluate your place.

DAY 7

Clean Up

The children's ministry director at another church in my town recently posted a picture on social media. I couldn't believe it when I saw it.

What was it?

It was a picture of a huge snakeskin that she found in the children's area of the church. Nothing says, "We'd love to have your kids join us at church this week!" like a picture of a snakeskin!

In the 1960s, a communication theorist named Marshall McLuhan said, "The medium is the message." He was pointing out the fact that everything you do (and don't do) communicates something to someone.

In his book, *The Tipping Point,* Malcolm Gladwell points out a social theory of crime called "The Broken Windows Theory." According to this theory, "Crime is the inevitable result of disorder. If a window is left broken and unrepaired, people walking by will conclude that no one cares and no one is in charge. Soon, more windows will be broken, and the sense of anarchy will spread from the building to the street on which it faces, sending a signal that anything goes."[10]

I'm not saying that if you don't clean up, then your students will become anarchists. I'm simply saying that **the place where your students meet communicates a message to them.**

That message might say, "We value you."

It might say, "We're not very interested in you."

Or, it might say, "We want new people to come." One of the easiest ways to communicate that you're expecting new students to show up is to clean up.

When you're hosting guests at your house, do you clean up? Of course you do! Even when those guests are friends, you still take a few minutes beforehand and put things away.

Every week, my wife and I host an adult small group at our house. These people have been to our house several times already. They're our friends. But we still make sure that everything is clean and organized before they arrive.

Why?

We clean up because we want them to know that they're important to us. We want them to know that we value what we're doing. If they came in and the house was a wreck, it would communicate that they were an interruption. They wouldn't feel welcome. We don't want them to feel like that, so we clean up. And it's even more important to clean up when you're hosting people that you've never met or don't know very well.

The same thing applies to the place where your students meet.

In his book, *Deep and Wide,* Andy Stanley says, "Every physical setting communicates something. There are no neutral settings. *Clean and tidy* communicates that you are expecting someone…When our church environments aren't clean, we are communicating something: 'We didn't think you were actually going to show up!'"[11]

If you want more students to show up, then you have to clean up. Clear out the clutter. Throw away the old papers and outdated event announcement cards. Get rid of the broken chairs. Spray some air freshener. Buy some Clorox wipes and scrub the tables.

Make it look like you're hosting an event for some very important people. After all, your students *are* very important people.

Today, your job is to clean up.

DAY 8

Invite an Interior Designer

I was standing in line at Chick-fil-A with one of my small group leaders when he said something that surprised me.

We had started talking about how much we like Chickfil-A. The food is great; the employees are friendly; the stores are clean. We always have a great experience there. Then he said something that caught me off guard.

"Do you know what I really like here?" he said.

"What?" I asked.

"I really like the new, white menu boards. They just look so clean and fresh." That surprised me.

This guy wasn't an interior designer; he was a teacher. But he still understood how colors, images, and textures on the walls and throughout the restaurant affect people.

He told me about the classroom he inherited when he was hired. It was filled with stuff. It had old pictures on the walls, old carpets on the floor, and old textbooks stacked on dusty shelves in the corner.

"It was depressing," he said. "Kids didn't want to be in there. It was a terrible learning environment."

So he cleaned it up and gave it a makeover.

One of the churches that I worked at had a student room with great potential. But when I showed up, it wasn't attractive to new students, much less our current students.

The paint was a dingy, white color with stains and cracks showing everywhere. Burgundy curtains were hanging over the windows. The light fixtures had a shiny brass finish. It felt like a banquet hall from the early 1990s.

The backdrop of the stage was filled with hand-painted words that reminded me of a middle school art project. There were group pictures from eight years earlier scattered in a random configuration on the walls. An old couch that someone had donated a decade ago greeted students as soon as they walked in the door.

The whole space needed a makeover.

I could see the problems, but I didn't know how to fix them. Seminary teaches you a lot about the Bible, but it doesn't teach you about interior design!

I knew I needed help, so I reached out to a friend who does interior design for Chick-fil-A. A few days later, she came out and looked at our space. She asked a few questions, drew a few diagrams, and made a few notes. Later that week, she sent me a detailed list of recommendations.

I met with the senior pastor to explain what changes I wanted to make and why I felt like it was necessary to make them. With his approval, my volunteers and I worked hard to give the room a makeover.

We took the old pictures down, painted the walls a new color, updated the light fixtures, switched out the furniture, and reset the room. The changes weren't very expensive, but they made a huge difference.

The students were blown away by the changes. The whole room felt fresh, vibrant, and comfortable. It made them happy to be there. Instead of being embarrassed to invite their friends to come to church with them, they felt empowered.

That wouldn't have happened without the help of an interior designer. Don't try to do this by yourself. And definitely don't rely on another pastor's wife to do it. If you don't take her suggestions, she might take it personally and the relationship will be awkward afterward.

I was fortunate to have a friend who did it for free. If you ask around, I'm sure you can find someone who knows an interior designer who will be glad to help you. It might cost a few hundred dollars, but when you see new students showing up at your church, you'll know that it was worth it!

Today, your job is to invite an interior designer to come and see your place.

DAY 9

Call a Larger Church

It's often said that larger churches have more resources, but smaller churches have better relationships. That's not entirely true.

In reality, the average person in any church knows around sixty other people in the church. The church could have 100 members or 1,000 attenders, but the fact remains that most people won't know more than sixty people.

What *is* true about that statement is that larger churches have more resources. I've worked at small churches and large churches, and I can confirm that larger churches have more stuff. That's for sure.

Larger churches also seem to change things more often. That means they get rid of stuff more quickly. Some of that stuff goes into a storage unit. Other stuff goes to the dumpster. And the things that get thrown away are sometimes better than what other churches are using every week.

This is especially true when it comes to stage designs and furniture. The old stuff has to go somewhere to make room for the new stuff.

I currently work at a large church. We change our stage designs three times every year: before the new year, after Easter, and before the new school year.

In order to build a new set, the old set has to be taken down. But we don't have any use for the old set anymore. We can't use it again because everyone has already seen it. We're usually left with no option other than to take those big pieces to the dumpster.

A few months ago, I received a phone call from a youth pastor at a smaller church in my area. He asked if we had anything we were planning to get rid of soon. He probably thought I was just sending him away, but I told him to give me some time to check around.

Four weeks later, we were changing out stage design and I thought of that youth pastor. I called him back and told him that he could have the whole set for free if he could come pick it up. His church had a van and a trailer, so he was thrilled with the offer.

A few hours later, he pulled in. I helped him load everything in the trailer and he was on his way. It was a win-win. We made room for the new stage design; he got an amazing set that is better than anything he could've created on his own.

But it wouldn't have happened if he hadn't asked.

Don't be ashamed or embarrassed to call a larger church and ask for stuff. You and I both know that sometimes the leftovers from a larger church are better than the best efforts of a smaller church. Don't let pride get in your way.

I've even heard of larger churches giving smaller churches projectors and sound equipment. They were in the middle of upgrading their stuff, and they thought it would be too complicated to sell it. Instead, they gave it away.

And who do you think they called?

They called the church that had reached out and expressed interest. They called the guys who put their pride aside and asked if there was anything they could have when they were done with it.

You might not have a large budget, but that doesn't mean you can't call a large church. You'll be told no a lot. But when one person calls you back and says he has something for you, you'll know it was worth it.

Today, your job is to call a larger church.

DAY 10

Set Up Snacks

Food makes people feel comfortable. I think it has something to do with having something to do.

When someone walks into a new place, they might feel self-conscious and exposed. They don't have anything to do, and they don't know what to do. They feel like an outsider who is out of place. In reality, no one probably notices them and they don't stand out at all, but they feel like everyone's eyes are on them because they're new.

Things change for that person when they're given something to drink and a snack to eat. All of a sudden they have something to do. They're not just standing there or aimlessly wandering around. Food even gives them an easy way to make conversation with someone else: "How about these snacks? They're good, aren't they?"

That's why food has been such a big part of showing hospitality for thousands of years. It makes people feel comfortable, safe, and connected. I think that's part of why Jesus ate with people so often. You'll remember, Jesus didn't try to change Zacchaeus on the spot; he ate with him first. Hospitality often precedes conversion.

When a new student walks into your room, he feels self-conscious and exposed. The way you help him feel comfortable, safe, and connected is by having snacks available. It doesn't have to be anything fancy or filling, just some light refreshments will do.

I recommend getting a few salty snacks and a few sweet ones. Doritos, Cheetos, and Famous Amos Cookies work well. Chewy candies like Starburst, Airheads, and even fruit snacks are usually popular with my students. So are hard candies like Blow Pops. Some of your students will have certain food allergies, so have something available for them too.

Also, I'd go with individually wrapped items, like the ones that moms pack in kids' lunches. That way you don't have a big bowl of leftover Chex Mix that you have throw out later. You can reuse those snack bags every week.

I also recommend using cans of soda and bottles of water instead of trying to pour from 2-liter bottles into plastic cups. Not only will you save yourself from having to clean up the mess when a seventh grade boy demonstrates his inability to pour, but you'll also be able to reuse the leftover drinks from week to week because they won't go flat.

You might be thinking, "My budget is small. How am I going to pay for all of that?"

If you have a small budget, I suggest you try three things:

46

1. Cut back in other areas.

Look over your expenses for the last three months to see if you're spending too much on something that isn't giving you a good return on investment. Stop spending your money on that and start setting up snacks instead.

2. Ask someone to pay for it.

Ask a parent, volunteer, or member of the church to pay for it. People like to give money to help with specific needs. All you have to do is explain why it matters and ask them to help you make it happen.

3. Create a café.

If you still can't find a way to give snacks away, then create a café. Buy the supplies, set up a spot in your room, make a price list, and find a volunteer to run it for you. Use the money that comes in to go back and buy more snacks. If you manage it right, it will pay for itself after a few weeks.

Food brings people together. Use it to bring your students together.

Today, your job is to set up snacks.

WEEK IN REVIEW

Day 6:

Evaluate your place. Students who visit your church usually decide whether or not they're going to come back before your program even starts.

Day 7:

Clean up. Make it look like you're hosting an event for some very important people. After all, your students *are* very important people.

Day 8:

Invite an interior designer. It might cost a few hundred dollars, but when you see new students showing up at your church, you'll know that it was worth it!

Day 9:

Call a larger church. You'll be told no a lot. But when one person calls you back and says he has something for you, you'll know it was worth it.

Day 10:

Set up snacks. Students who walk into your room feel self-conscious and exposed. Food and drinks help them feel comfortable, safe, and connected.

PART 3:
Paying Attention to Your Programs

Creating Events That Engage Students

DAY 11

Evaluate Your Programs

I like how Kurt Johnston defines programs. He says, "Programs = The Stuff Your Ministry Does...Every ministry does stuff, and the stuff you do can accurately be defined as programs."[12]

A few months ago, I received a call from a guy who wanted to talk about his church's youth ministry. He was concerned that they weren't on the right track.

I asked him to tell me about their programs. I wanted to know when they meet, what they do when they meet, and what they were trying to accomplish by meeting.

He told me that they meet on Sunday mornings, Sunday nights, and Wednesday nights. I asked him to describe a typical Sunday night. He couldn't do it. He said that sometimes they do a Bible study, and sometimes they just don't meet at all.

I asked him to describe a typical Wednesday night. Again, he couldn't do it. He said that sometimes a guy plays a few songs on his guitar, and sometimes they just sit around and talk.

I asked him to describe what usually happens on a Sunday morning. He said that sometimes they meet in groups according to grade and gender, and sometimes they just sit around and eat muffins.

The key word that he kept using was "sometimes." Sometimes they do this. Sometimes they do that. The problem was a lack of consistency. Students didn't know what to expect from week to week. Neither did the volunteers. And it's hard to get excited about something when you don't know what will be happening when you get there.

The deeper problem was that they hadn't taken the time to figure out who they were trying to reach and what they hoped to accomplish by meeting. The answers to those questions would clarify what they needed to do in each program.

Here's an exercise for you to do today:

Take out a sheet of paper and look at last month's calendar. Write down all of the times when students are expected to meet.

Now, for each of those times, write down who the target audience is for that program. Who are you trying to reach during that time? Is the program designed to educate Christian students? Is it designed to build a sense of unity and friendship among your regular attenders? Is it designed to appeal to non-Christian students?

All of those are valid aims, but they're very difficult to accomplish at the same time. You need to identify who you're trying to reach and what you're trying to accomplish with everything on your calendar.

If you're not sure how to decide who the target audience is for a program, then try to answer this question: If a student who regularly attends your church wanted to invite one of their non-Christian friends to come, which program would they invite their friend to attend?

I recently stopped by another youth ministry in my area to observe a Wednesday night program. While I was there, I asked a high school student that question. He said that he would most likely invite a friend to attend on a Sunday morning. That stuck out to me because he should've said Wednesday night. In that youth ministry's strategy, Wednesday night was supposed to be the best time for students to invite their friends.

There was a bit of distance between what that youth pastor thought should be happening and what was actually happening.

Now that you've written down what should be happening in your programs, it's time for a few followup questions:

- *Is there a balance between reaching outsiders and strengthening insiders?*
- *Are the programs connecting with their target audience?*
- *Are the programs accomplishing their intended goals?*
- *Are students being encouraged and equipped to take the next step in their faith?*

- *What could be added or eliminated to more effectively accomplish the goal for each program?*

When you have those answers, you're ready to move ahead.

Today, your job is to evaluate your programs.

DAY 12

Make a Plan

Students can tell when you haven't planned the program. It doesn't start on time. It doesn't end on time. There are gaps with awkward silence. People aren't in the right places. Nothing is ready, and nothing goes right. That doesn't make a student want to come back next week.

On the other hand, students can also tell when you've prepared. They can tell when you have a plan for your program. It starts on time. It ends on time. People are in the right places. The segments flow together seamlessly.

When you prepare, it shows you care.

You are showing the students that you care about them when you take the time to put together a plan for your program. You're also showing them that you value your time together. *If you believe that what you're doing is important, then you should take the time to plan for it*

I want you to focus your attention this week on your large group program. I know that you have other programs; you should make a plan for those too. But if your large group program isn't done well, then you won't be able to reach new students who will eventually be interested in those other things.

There are 7 parts to your large group program:

1. Pre-Service

2. Hosting

3. Game

4. Songs

5. Message

6. Response

7. Dismissal

Every one of these parts is important, so it's important for you to think through each one. It's also important for you to know how you will move into and out of each one.

I suggest making a written plan for your program. Treat it like an event. When you attend a wedding, you receive a bulletin when you arrive that lists the order of service. Nothing is left to chance. Everything is planned out in advance.

If you attend a wedding and the pastor looks around and says, "Well, what's next?" you would be shocked. That's because people plan every detail when it comes to big events. They want everything to feel just right.

Your program is no different. It's an event. That's why you should make a written plan that covers all the details. You don't have to hand out a bulletin, but you should have printed copies available for people who have specific responsibilities.

Some people use a simple Word document for their written plan. Others use more technical tools, like Planning Center (see planningcenteronline.com). The key is to **write down what's happening and when it's happening.**

Here's an example:

6:00

Start pre-service playlist and slides

6:28

Play 2-minute countdown video

6:30

Welcome

Talk about weird news events from last week

Game

Mixer Question (while band loads on stage)

6:45

3 songs (worship leader prays at the end)

7:00

Message Bumper Video

Message

7:25

Response Time

7:30

Announcements

Dismissal

Do you see how a plan helps keep the program on track?

The person running the soundboard will know what's going on. The person in charge of the slides will know what's coming next. The students will be engaged the whole time because you've planned to keep their attention.

The important part of planning your program is to **keep things moving.** You don't want to stay in one part too long because your students have a short attention span.

You should change up what you're doing every 10 minutes or so. If you don't, you'll lose them. They'll start having side conversations. Or they'll pull out their phones and scroll through Instagram to see what their friends are doing.

Start with lots of fun to fill the room with energy and excitement. Then, with the music and message, you want to slowly move them toward a moment of contemplation in which they're ready to respond in the way God is leading them. After that, send them out on a high note. Tell them what's coming up in the next few weeks and turn on some feel-good music while they wait for their parents to pick them up.

When you do this consistently, students will show up consistently.

Today, your job is to make a plan.

DAY 13

Take Fun Seriously

My seminary didn't teach any courses about how to help students have fun at church.

New Testament survey? Yes.

Theology? Yes.

Church History? Yes.

Fun? No.

I was at a youth ministry conference where I overheard a youth pastor talking with one of the speakers. The youth pastor described his situation: he was teaching his heart out every week, but no one new was coming. Worse still, the students who did show up, just looked at him with blank stares and bored faces.

The speaker candidly asked if they were doing anything fun to engage his students and attract new ones. After a few seconds of silence, the youth pastor quietly responded, "Well, no. I didn't think it was *that* important."

Don't make that mistake.

You need to take fun seriously. **Helping your students have fun at church is one of your highest priorities.**

There are three reasons why that's true:

1. Students want to have fun.

Reggie Joiner says, "We were made to have fun." We all want to have a good time. We all want to laugh and enjoy ourselves. It isn't just students who like to have fun; it's everyone!

Fun matters. There's no distinction between Christian and non-Christian students when it comes to fun: every student wants to have fun.

2. Students will come back for fun.

There are tremendous pressures on students today. They feel pressure to make good grades, pressure to fit in, pressure to stand out, pressure to excel. In the midst of those pressures, students are looking for a place where they can simply enjoy themselves and have fun. And when they find a place like that, they'll come back for more.

We all know the story:

A guy spends the night with a friend. He wakes up on Sunday morning and goes to another church with his friend. That church was fun. It was more fun than your church. Next thing you know, he's begging his parents to go to the new church. Eventually, that family leaves your church and starts attending the other one. When students have fun, they'll want to come back.

3. Students will invite their friends to something fun.

Because students want to have fun, and will come back for fun, they will also invite their friends to share in the fun.

Students are like pack animals: they never want to be alone. That's why they'll instinctively invite their friends to something they think is worth being at. You don't have to beg them to invite friends; they do it naturally.

If they think you'll embarrass them, they *won't* invite their friends. If they think your program isn't good, they *won't* invite their friends. But if they think something fun is happening, they *will* invite friends. That's how it works.

Here's an equation I want you to understand:

MORE FUN = MORE STUDENTS

It's that simple. Your seminary professor didn't tell you, but helping students have fun at church is one of your highest priorities if you want them to come back and invite their friends.

Today, your job is to take fun seriously.

DAY 14

Create a Song List

A few years ago, we had to wait until the next Passion Conference to get our hands on new worship music. Guys like Chris Tomlin, Matt Redman, and David Crowder would all reveal their newest material at the conference each year. Then, when the album finally came out, student worship bands across the country all worked overtime to be able to play those new songs as soon as possible.

Those songs sustained many youth ministries for the next twelve months until the next album was released after the next Passion Conference. Students learned those words, and those words sunk deep into their hearts and minds. Just the other night, I was cooking dinner for my family. Out of nowhere, I started to sing, "You are the Lord, the Famous One, Famous One. Great is Your Name in all the earth." That song came out in 2002!

Today, it seems like new worship songs come out every

week. When you get ready to plan the music for your program, you aren't just looking at a list of fifteen songs, you're looking at fifty songs.

I think the temptation is to phase out old songs and phase in new songs too quickly. Then we wonder why our students aren't singing. They aren't singing because people can't sing a song they don't know. They can say the words, but it takes a few repetitions before they can sing it from the heart.

Here's what typically happens:

We introduce new songs to our students. It takes a few weeks, but they begin to learn them. They start to sing along. And then, many times, just when they're beginning to really engage with God through those songs, we move on to other new songs.

We move too quickly. Those songs haven't had the chance to make a deep impression on our students yet. They won't be making dinner one night when they're 30 years old and spontaneously think of those songs. To fight against that temptation, I suggest that you create a song list for each semester. This is an idea that I picked up from Todd Fields, the Director of Worship Leader Development at North Point Community Church.

Before the semester starts, pick fifteen songs that you think your students will connect with. You'll want to classify them according to theme and tempo so you don't end up with too many slow songs or not enough reflective songs on the list. Ideally, you can look at your teaching calendar (see Day 17) and select songs with lyrics that highlight the themes you'll be talking about.

Remember: Just because your musicians are getting tired of playing a song, doesn't mean you should move it out of the rotation for the next semester. In fact, when your musicians get tired of playing a song, your students have probably just started to engage with it.

That's not to say that you should never move on to new songs. You should introduce new songs a couple of times each year, but you shouldn't introduce too many at one time.

Todd Fields suggests four categories to use when considering what to do with songs:

1. Keep the ones that are hits.

2. Review the ones that are new.

3. Pause the ones that are stale.

4. Remove the ones that are old.

As an added benefit, when you create a song list for the semester, your musicians will play better because they will have more practice playing the songs together. Instead of having to learn new songs each week, they'll be able to perfect the ones they already know. Your students will notice the increase in quality.

When your students are singing songs they know, they won't have to focus on reading the words off the screen. When your musicians are playing songs they know, they won't have to focus on reading the words off the music stand. That will free up both your students and your musicians to focus on the God they're singing about.

Today, your job is to create a song list.

DAY 15

Do a Run-Through

This is something that I learned about when I joined the staff of a North Point Strategic Partner church.

My previous experience had been at a smaller, traditional church. We didn't run through anything. We just did it. That created some awkward moments in our services, but we didn't know it could be any different.

North Point doesn't operate like that. **Every part of the service is planned for and practiced before it's performed.** We call it a run-through.

A run-through is the equivalent of a dress rehearsal for a theater performance.

A few years ago, my wife and I went to see an offBroadway production of the The Lion King. She had a friend who was involved with the show, so we were able to go a day early and check things out.

When we walked into the auditorium, the music was blasting and performers were acting out their parts as if the place were filled with people. They were in the middle of a dress rehearsal. It was a show before the show.

What's the point of a run-through?

A run-through is important for three reasons. One reason is to make sure everyone understands what's happening. There are several people involved in your program: someone runs sound, someone runs slides, the band plays music, and someone gets up to speak.

If any one of those people isn't fully aware of what's happening and what's next, then the service can go from smooth to shaky in a hurry. A run-through helps everyone get a feel for how the program is supposed to flow.

A second reason to do a run-through is that it allows you to work through transitions. How will you get your game supplies in position at the right time? How will the band know when to come on stage? How will you move from the music to the message? How will you end the service?

All of those are points of transition in your program. If they aren't handled well, then you'll lose the attention of your students. A run-through helps everyone understand how the transitions will work so nothing gets lost in the turns.

The third reason is practice. Everyone feels more comfortable after they've done something the first time. That's the point of practice.

There's a big difference between going over your message in your head or in the shower and delivering it out loud on the stage. Sometimes, the joke you came up with by yourself in the car sounded a lot better in your mind than it does in the actual service. You want to find that out before the room is filled with students.

A run-through can be the difference between creating events that engage students and creating events that bore students. It allows you to get the right things right and remove the things that don't belong.

In a run-through, you run through everything in real time, at full speed, so everyone understands what's supposed to happen before it happens.

Doing a run-through will require you and your team to show up earlier, but the result is that your program will be better and your students will show up more often. I think it's a good trade.

Today, your job is to do a run-through.

WEEK IN REVIEW

Day 11:

Evaluate your programs. If a student who regularly attends your church wanted to invite one of their nonChristian friends to come, which program would they invite their friend to attend?

Day 12:

Make a plan. You show the students that you care about them when you take the time to put together a plan for your program.

Day 13:

Take fun seriously. If students think something fun is happening at your church, they will invite friends.

Day 14:

Create a song list. You should introduce new songs a couple of times each year, but you shouldn't introduce too many at one time.

Day 15:

Do a run-through. Take the time to run through everything in real time, at full speed, so everyone understands what's supposed to happen before it happens.

PART 4:
Paying Attention
to Your Preaching

Crafting Messages
That Help Students

DAY 16

Evaluate Your Preaching

Thom Rainer has done extensive research on church growth and revitalization. In his book, *Surprising Insights from the Unchurched and Proven Ways to Reach Them,* he explains how preaching is one of the most important reasons why people attend the churches they do.

He writes, "We asked the open ended question, 'What factors led you to choose this church?' The responses... show that facts related to the pastor and preaching were the most-often mentioned answers."[13]

Even though his research is primarily focused on adults, I think the responses from students would be similar. If you want to build a better youth ministry, you have to pay attention to what you say and how you say it.

The first step to becoming a better speaker is to evaluate your preaching. And there's a simple way to do it: record yourself.

Somewhere along the way, I think we've all heard this advice. What shocks me is how few of us actually do it.

I think most people avoid this simple advice because there's something about our own voices that makes us uncomfortable.

The first time I ever spoke at a church they gave me a cassette tape of my message. My excitement turned to horror when I listened to it. I talked too fast. I didn't make a clear point. I rambled a lot. There wasn't a solid call to action. It was bad. I was uncomfortable. But it made me better.

My habit now is to listen to my sermon on the way home after church. I like to listen immediately afterward because everything is still fresh in my mind at that point. I can still see myself saying those words. I can still see the students' faces when I told a story or explained a certain part of a verse. If I let a few days go by, then I'll lose the connection to those moments and the evaluation won't be as accurate.

Sometimes, I find that I did better than I originally thought I did. Other times, I find that I wasn't as clear as I originally thought I was. The recording doesn't lie. Every time I listen, I find something that I can do better next time.

If you want to take it a step further, then consider making a video. A video recording is even better than an audio recording. This doesn't require high-tech video equipment. A simple flip cam or smart phone can work fine.

TJ Walker, CEO of Media Training Worldwide, says, "You have to see video of yourself speaking if you want to improve, and there is absolutely no excuse not to do so."[14]

Here are a few questions to consider as you listen or watch:

- *Are you expressing emotion or are you monotone?*
- *Are you enunciating your words so people can understand you?*
- *Are you using filler words (um, uh, etc)?*
- *How is your speed: Too fast? Too slow?*
- *How is your volume: Too soft? Too loud?*
- *How is your tone: Too passive? Too aggressive?*
- *How is your body language: Nervous? Confident?*
- *Is there a strong opening that creates intrigue?*
- *Is there a clear bottom line?*
- *Is there a clear next action step for people to take?*
- *If you were a student, would you say this message is helpful?*

If you don't have a recording, then today I just want you to think back to your last message and ask these questions. It's hard to evaluate your own preaching, but it's possible if you can remain objective in the process. Most of the speakers that I know have a tendency to overestimate their preaching skills. They aren't hard enough on themselves because they know how hard they worked on the message. If you can't be objective, then ask someone else to evaluate your preaching. Either way, today your job is to evaluate your preaching.

DAY 17

Create a Teaching Calendar

One of the hardest parts of speaking every week is deciding what to say. It's so hard because there are so many topics, themes, and texts that you want your students to learn about, and your time with them is so short.

It's not a new problem. Charles Spurgeon, the great 19th century British preacher, admitted, "My text selection is a very great embarrassment. There are so many truths, all clamoring for a hearing, so many duties all needing enforcing, and so many spiritual needs of the people all demanding supply. I confess that I frequently sit hour after hour praying and waiting for a subject, and that this is the main part of my study."[15]

Maybe you sense that same overwhelming feeling as you prepare your message each week. A teaching calendar will make that anxiety go away because you won't be scrambling at the last minute trying to figure out what you're talking about. It will already be written down.

Here's what you need to do:

1. List the dates.

Create a document and list every Sunday or Wednesday (depending on when you speak) for the next 6 months. I do this in Evernote, but you can do it with a Google document or Excel sheet if you want to. The key is to get the dates written down so you can see what's coming.

2. Think about the seasons.

There are times in the year when people are more likely to come to your church for the first time. In my experience, more new students and families attend in January and August than any other months. Also, Easter Sunday is usually the highest attended Sunday of the year.

There are also times in the year when people are less likely to attend. June and July are usually the months with the lowest attendance. Students are out of school, families go away for vacation, and sometimes they just stay home and enjoy the warm weather.

There are also busy seasons in your church. In many churches, November and December are busy months. Some people go out of town for Thanksgiving. Some are just worn out from decorating and shopping for Christmas. Students' schedules are usually filled with homework, projects, tests and exams as the semester comes to an end. Everyone is busy.

As you look at the dates, pay attention to Hallmark holidays too. According to Wikipedia, these are the days that exist primarily for commercial purposes, rather than to commemorate any traditionally significant event. These are days like Valentine's Day, Mother's Day, and Father's Day.

3. Think about the students.

In marketing, there are two ways to analyze customers: demographics and psychographics. Demographics analyzes externals. It looks at things like age, race, family size, and household income. Psychographics analyzes internals. It looks at things like values, lifestyles, interests, hurts, and fears.

For your teaching calendar, you want to focus on psychographics. Rick Warren says, "You need to discover how they think. What are their interests? What do they value? Where do they hurt? …What are their most popular radio stations? The more you know about these
people, the easier it will be to reach them."[16]

Here's a simple question that will help you think about your students:

"What is it like to be _____?"

You could say, "What is it like to be a 7th grade girl?" "What is it like to be a student with a part-time job?" Even better, you could fill in the blank with an actual student's name from your group: "What is it like to be Brian?" The more specific you get, the more you'll be able to connect with your students, and the better your messages will be.

4. Think about the sermons.

With the seasons and students in the front of your mind, start writing down topics, themes, and texts that you want to teach about.

I recommend packaging your sermons in a series. That will allow you to build momentum and anticipation from one week to the next. It also gives your students an easy opportunity to invite their friends because they'll know what you're going to talk about. I wouldn't make any series longer than four weeks. Even if your content is fresh and new, it will begin to feel tired and old after several weeks of the same packaging.

Don't worry about naming your messages or series yet. You can go back and do that later. You probably want to invite a few other creative people into that process anyway. For now, just get the topics, themes, and texts written down. This will help you plan ahead and begin to collect stories, illustrations, and ideas ahead of time instead of scrambling two days before you're supposed to speak.

Today, your job is to create a teaching calendar.

DAY 18

Make Your Moves

Every message has a structure. It might be tight and thought out. Or it might be loose and impromptu. Either way, there is a structure.

A sermon is a series of moves that build on each other. You say something. Then you say something else. Then you say something else. And eventually, you're done.

In his book, *Homiletic,* David Buttrick explains, "A sermon, any sermon, will involve a sequence of subject matters – simple meanings – arranged in some sort of structural design. Each simple meaning will be developed into a move – a language module between three and four minutes long."[17]

Every message you preach is built on a series of sequential moves. How you make your moves will determine whether or not your students will listen to and learn from what you say.

Many preachers lose people from the start because they assume their audience cares what they're getting ready to say. You know they have this assumption because the first move in their message is to introduce the Bible text. They begin by announcing, "The sermon today comes from John 14:1-6." Then they read the text aloud and start unpacking it. Eventually, they'll finish with some do's and don'ts that people should consider.

I think that's the wrong assumption today. It might have been okay forty years ago, but not today. In a postChristian society, many students have no reverence for the Bible. They don't see any reason why the Bible should have privileged status among every other book. To begin with the Bible is to assume it has authority in their eyes. That's an assumption we can no longer make with today's students.

I'm not saying that you shouldn't use the Bible for your sermons. I'm just saying that you shouldn't begin with it. Instead, here are the moves you should make in your messages and the order I think you should make them:

1. Create Common Ground.

Students have to believe the messenger before they'll believe the message. This is your chance to show them you're not that different from them.

Talk about your struggles with the topic you're covering. Talk about your successes with it. Tell a story about an event where you encountered it head-on. Transparency leads to trust, so if you want your students to trust you then you have to be transparent from the start.

2. Build the Tension.

People learn on a need-to-know basis. If they don't think your topic matters for them right now, then they'll tune you out and starting checking their social media feed.

You want to create as much tension as you can for as many people as possible.

Andy Stanley says, "Assume no interest. Focus on the question you are intending to answer until you are confident your audience wants it answered. Otherwise you are about to spend twenty or thirty minutes of your life answering a question nobody is asking."[18]

When you build the tension, you're raising the questions that raise the stakes that your topic has in students' lives.

3. Open the Bible.

After you've sparked their interest, it's time to point them to what God says about the topic. You don't need to mention every passage that addresses the topic; just pick one and stay there. Be sure to point out and explain any words or concepts that might be unfamiliar or hard to understand.

You want to make the Bible as engaging as you can for students. Tell them about the background. Give them the context. Help them understand what's happening in the scene. Who are the characters? Where are they? What's going on? Why does it matter?

4. Reveal the Big Idea.

The Big Idea is your sermon in a sentence. It's your central point. It's the statement you want your students remember. When they get in the car and their parents ask them what they learned, you want them to be able to say this statement. When they get home, you want them to tweet this statement.

Steve Jobs was a master at this. In his book, *The Presentation Secrets of Steve Jobs,* Carmine Gallo says, "Jobs creates headlines that are specific, are memorable, and best of all, can fit on a Twitter post."[19] Your big idea should be a tweetable statement of 140 characters or less.

One of my favorite Big Ideas came in a message about serving. I said, *"Students who serve are students who stay."* That line is specific, memorable, and tweetable. It takes some work, but it's worth the effort to come up with a statement that sticks.

5. Suggest Next Action Steps.

No message is complete without offering students a few ways to put the information into action. You need to tell them what to do with what they've heard. This is where you answer the question, "Now what?"

Consider the different categories of students: some are **skeptical** about faith, some are **struggling** with faith, and some are **strong** in their faith. It's possible that each group might have a different next action step. You aren't telling them what to do; you're just suggesting practical ways for them to put their faith into action.

When it comes to length, I don't see any reason why your sermon should take more than 20 minutes to deliver. You should spend three to four minutes on each move. If someone can explain neuroscience in an 18-minute TED Talk, then you should be able to get through your message in approximately that amount of time too. Besides, students have short attention spans.

Preaching isn't just about what you say. It's also about *how* you say it. You can tell your students lots of things that are true, but if you deliver those truths in a way that doesn't energize and empower them to do something about it then your preaching won't make much of an impact on their lives.

Today, your job is to make your moves.

DAY 19

Get a Stool

Long before *Newsweek* honored Fred Craddock as one of America's top preachers, and shortly before he joined the faculty of Candler School of Theology, he wrote a book called, *As One Without Authority* It was 1971, but he already saw a major shift happening that would affect the future of preaching.

What did he see?

It wasn't just the Bible that was losing authority among people; *preachers were losing authority too.*

He said, "An examination of great evangelistic sermons of the past makes it clear that the speaker assumed at the outset that the hearers were part of a culture that was Christian and the appeal to them was simply not to be 'holdouts.' This condition is rapidly disappearing, and the claim of the gospel must be presented on its own terms with the understanding that the hearers stand amid several alternatives."[20]

According to a Pew Research Study in 2014, the "Nones"

are on the rise.[21] "Nones" are people who identify as either atheist or agnostic, or who claim no religion at all.

Thirty-five percent of Millennials identify are already in that category, and the number is trending up. Not only that, the "Nones" are also getting younger.

Here's what all of this means:

Neither the Bible's words nor your words have automatic authority for today's students.

If you get on a stage, stand behind a table, and talk down to students, your words will fall on deaf ears. That posture assumes the authority that came with the position forty years ago. But times have changed.

A study published in the *Review of Religious Research* found that when the audience believes the speaker is kind, likeable, and understanding, they will seriously consider his views – even if they're different from their own.[22]

If you talk down to your students and present the biblical version of reality as if it's the only one that's available, then your students will tune you out. It feels narrowminded and it doesn't meet them where they are.

On the other hand, if you talk openly with your students and present the biblical version of reality over against the other options in the marketplace of ideas, then they'll tune into what you have to say. They'll feel like you "get" them.

Your message should feel more like a conversation than a lecture. In their book, *Speaking to Teenagers,* Doug Fields and Duffy Robbins pointed this out. They advised,

"*Be conversational* Teenagers are much more responsive to someone who's *talking to them* than they are to someone who's *giving a talk at them*"[23]

When you speak to students, your tone and demeanor should be like you're sitting with them in the booth at a restaurant. You wouldn't rant and rave in a restaurant, would you? I hope not. Instead, you would have a thoughtful, deliberate conversation that honored the other person's feelings and current situation. That's the way you should preach to students today.

I believe the simplest way to reinforce this posture is to **get a stool.** Instead of standing up and delivering your words of wisdom from "on high," you should take a seat and create a sense of conversation. When you sit down to speak, you communicate a sense of intimacy and transparency that will help your students open up to and engage with your message.

Your sermon should feel more like, "Here's what I see" and "Here's what I'm thinking," and less like, "Here's how it is" and "Here's where you're wrong."

Does the Bible have authority for Christians? Yes.

Should you have authority in your church? Yes. Ideally, your students will recognize and respond to both your authority and the Bible's authority. But we don't live in an ideal world. We live in the real world. And here in the real world, you have to speak as one without authority.

Think of yourself like a missionary in a foreign land. Missionaries don't give lectures; they have conversations. They honor the people they're talking with. They don't assume the high ground. They discuss the options and make a compelling case for the validity of the gospel among the alternative options. That's what you have to do when you speak to your students.

Today, your job is to get a stool.

DAY 20

Schedule a Guest Speaker

Crafting messages that help students is hard work. It takes a lot of time and creativity to come up with introductions that intrigue, stories that connect, and applications that empower.

Because of that, camp speakers and evangelists have an advantage over youth pastors. Those guys are able to use the same messages and illustrations every week because they're talking to different groups. After they speak, they're able to tweak their content and delivery to make it even better the next time.

For the youth pastor, there isn't a next time. After you present a message, it's over. Can you imagine the uproar that would happen if you pulled out a sermon from three weeks ago and preached it again this week? You'd never hear the end of it!

You're expected to be fresh and funny, clear and convincing, informative and inspiring every week. As if that weren't hard enough to do by itself, speaking isn't your only job. You're also supposed to lead volunteers, plan events, communicate with parents, go to students' school events, and contribute in staff meetings.

There simply isn't enough time to be great at everything every week. You cannot deliver fifty-two meaningful, memorable messages every year. And yet, many youth pastors are expected to do twice that many because their students meet more than once a week.

But it can't happen.

You get tired. Your creativity runs dry. You wake up in a rut. You get sick. Things happen and you get pulled away from message preparation to handle other issues in the church. And your messages in those weeks leave a lot to be desired.

Andy Stanley is considered by many people to be a great preacher. Thousands of people think so highly of his messages that they show up at church just to see a video of him preaching. But, as good as Andy Stanley is, he doesn't speak every week. In fact, I would say that one of the reasons he *can* be so good when he speaks is precisely because he doesn't speak every week.

According to the message archive on www.northpoint.org, Andy delivered 34 messages in 2015. That's 65% of the Sundays. Granted, he also spoke at several other events outside of Sunday morning, but that's not the point. The point is that someone other than Andy Stanley preached 35% of the Sunday sermons at his church.

Why would he do that?

I think there are at least three reasons:

1. Quality

Again, you simply can't be at your best every week. Taking a few weeks off from speaking allows you to create great content and be at your best the next time you speak.

2. Growth

Weekly routines can easily become weekly ruts. Time off from speaking gives you the space you need to discover, learn about, and experiment with new ideas.

3. Perspective

Things look different on the stage when you aren't part of them. When you participate in the service like every other attender, you see things that you couldn't see otherwise.

If you want to have better perspective, experience personal growth, and increase the quality of your messages, then you have to step out and allow someone else to step in. Plus, your students will probably benefit by hearing from someone other than you all the time.

There are several ways you can do this. The simplest way is to invite someone else to speak. You could use one of your volunteers. You could ask another youth pastor. You could invite a teacher from a local Christian school. You could even ask your senior pastor.

Another way to have someone else speak for you is to use a video. The XP3 Curriculum from Orange is great for this. They include Communicator Videos for each series they produce. It's just one of their staff members delivering the message, but they include multiple camera angles and text on the screen that keeps students engaged the whole time.

When you take a week off, you'll find that you're more refreshed and better prepared the next time you speak. And that's important both for you and your students.

Today, your job is to schedule a guest speaker.

WEEK IN REVIEW

Day 16:

Evaluate your preaching. The first step to becoming a better speaker is to evaluate your preaching. And there's a simple way to do it: record yourself.

Day 17:

Create a teaching calendar. A teaching calendar will keep you from scrambling at the last minute trying to figure out what you're talking about.

Day 18:

Make your moves. How you structure your message will determine whether or not your students will listen to and learn from what you say.

Day 19:

Get a stool. If you get on a stage, stand behind a table, and talk down to students, your words will fall on deaf ears.

Day 20:

Schedule a guest speaker. If you want to have better perspective, experience personal growth, and increase the quality of your messages, then you have to step out and allow someone else to step in.

PART 5:

Paying Attention to Your People

*Getting Volunteers
Who Care About Students*

DAY 21

Evaluate Your People

It's been over a decade since Jim Collins wrote *Good to Great* He and his research team sought to uncover the key characteristics of companies that turned the corner from achieving adequate results to operating at levels of peak performance.

Collins explains, "The [leaders] who ignited the transformations from good to great did not first figure out where to drive the bus and then get people to take it there. No, they *first* got the right people on the bus (and the wrong people off the bus) and *then* figured out where to drive it."[24]

This concept has become commonplace in businesses across the country, but it's still catching on in churches.

Some of your volunteers have been faithful, but they've lost their passion. They need a break. But they feel like they're locked in. They would like to step down, but they don't know how.

They aren't the people you need on the bus right now. They're done.

Other volunteers are rock stars. They show up with lots of energy and enthusiasm. They love students and they love making a difference.

They are the people you want on your team. They're dedicated.

Most of the time you can spot who's engaged and who isn't. Watch for the signs:

- *Who shows up on time?*
- *Who show up prepared?*
- *Who knows the students' names?*
- *Who knows what's going on in students' lives?*
- *Who is willing to go the extra mile to make a difference?*

The people who come to mind when you answer those questions are the people you need on your team. Students respond to those kinds of volunteers. Plus, they're usually a lot of fun to be around!

Take some time to evaluate your current group of volunteers. Take them breakfast, lunch, or coffee. Have a heart-to-heart conversation about how they're doing and how things are going in the ministry.

Find out if they know what their role is. Ask them if they feel like they have the tools and the margin necessary to do a good job.

Sometimes people just need encouragement. Maybe they need training. Other times they just need a break. You need to find out which volunteers are in each category.

One of the hardest things to do is tell a volunteer that you think it'd be best if they volunteered in another ministry. But that's what you have to do if you care about your students and your ministry. Leaders make hard decisions, and they have hard conversations. Your church hired you to lead your ministry.

However, if you sense that a particular volunteer isn't living up to the commitment they made at the start, then letting them go might be easier than you think. Sometimes all it takes is a simple email that lets them off the hook.

Here's an example that has worked for me on more than one occasion:

Hi Ashley,

I wanted to check in with you re: being a small group leader Here's the thing: I want our small groups to be the best they can be Ultimately, those relationships are what make students want to come back week after week I've noticed that your presence in the group has been pretty inconsistent lately I totally understand that things come up and people have to be out, but we need to have small group leaders who are consistently pouring into students' lives to make this work

Here's what I want you to consider:

1)   Is this still a good season of life for you to be a small group leader?

2)   Are you able to commit to being present (physically, mentally, emotionally, and spiritually) for the students in your group?

If the answers to those questions are yes, then that's great! You know what it takes to have a great group, and

I think you're perfectly capable of building one If the answers those questions are no, then I think it's time to consider a new role for a while

I just want you to consider it You're a valuable member of what we're doing, but I don't want you to feel like you have to be locked in to leading a small group if it's not a good season right now Either way, I understand Just let me know what you think

In case you're wondering, Ashley replied to that email by saying: "My life is a little hectic right now. I love the ministry, but you're right. It might not be the best season of life right now. I need to step down. Thanks for being so understanding."

She is now happily serving in another ministry area that requires less commitment, and I've been able to replace her with someone who is passionate about students and has the margin in her life to be there in the small group. It's a win-win.

Today, your job is to evaluate your people.

DAY 22

Assign Roles and Goals

Your volunteers are with you because they want to make a difference with students.

Maybe their life was changed as a teenager when someone first told them about Jesus. Maybe they made mistakes as a student and they want to help the next generation of students avoid those mistakes. Maybe they remember their parents helping with students when they were growing up and now they feel like it's the right thing to do.

Whatever the reason, they're with you now.

They want to do a good job. They want to experience success. They want to win. But if they don't know exactly what you want them to do, then they'll make it up as they go along.

It's like Andy Stanley says:

"Without clear direction, they are forced to chart their own course or follow whoever seems to have the best plan at the moment."[25]

Oftentimes, volunteers will revert back to how they've seen it done before.

What your volunteers need from you is clarity around their roles and goals. They need you to tell them what they're supposed to do and what translates into points on the scoreboard.

Every volunteer position in your ministry needs a clear job description. The shorter it is, the better it is. You should try to get it down to one sentence if you can because a sentence is memorable, three pages aren't.

Sure, there are particular details that they'll need to know about policies and procedures, but don't clutter the job description with those. Just state what the job requires and be done.

Someone on your host team shouldn't be distracted with meaningless jargon and endless bullet points. Just tell them that you want them in place to help students feel welcomed and excited about what's happening before the program starts. That means they need to be in place, smiling, and greeting students as they arrive.

That's a one-sentence description that is clear and to the point.

You want to boil each role down to its simplest actions so your volunteers will remain focused on the right target.

Not only does having clear roles and goals help your volunteers experience the satisfaction of success, they also encourage your volunteers to stick around.

To quote Andy Stanley one more time:

"Our experience is that most volunteers…just want to know where to get in line so they can help. But if they are allowed to wander in the wrong direction for long, most volunteers will ultimately give up."[26]

When people know what's expected of them, they're able to do it and experience the satisfaction of a job well done. When you clarify roles and goals, your volunteers will do a better job and stay on your team longer. New faces become familiar faces, and familiar faces become trusted faces.

That trust turns into longevity, and longevity among your volunteers translates into huge gains for your ministry as time goes by.

Today, your job is to assign roles and goals.

DAY 23

Create a Process

If you want to get the right people on your team and keep the wrong people off your team, then you need to create a process that gives you time to learn about people and gives them time to learn about your ministry. You need an orientation process.

You want to make sure someone is a good fit and understands what they're committing to before you assign them a role in your ministry. It's easier to steer someone away before they get started than to let them go afterward.

We've all had people say they want to volunteer with students only to leave us hanging a few months later. When you're finally able to catch up with them, they apologize and explain how it just wasn't what they were looking for. That kind of turnover hurts your ministry's credibility with both students and parents, so you want to avoid it all costs.

When it comes to selecting volunteers, you're looking for 4 C's:

Character

Is this person in a growing relationship with Jesus Christ?

Competence

Does this person have the skills and experience to work with students?

Culture

Does this person embrace the mission, vision, and strategy of the church?

Chemistry

Will this person be a positive addition to the team?

In order to find out the answers to these questions, you need to take a little time to get to know someone. Spending this time is good for you and your students, as well as the potential volunteer. Plus, it communicates to people that you aren't desperate for volunteers. You want high-performing volunteers and desperation isn't attractive to those kinds of people.

This is the orientation process that I use:

Step 1: Volunteer Application & Background Check

It doesn't matter if I recruit someone to volunteer or they approach me about potential opportunities. Every volunteer fills out an application and authorizes a background check. The background check is how you keep your students safe, and the application is where you get key information about potential volunteers.

You want to include key questions like:

When and how did you become a Christian?

Have you ever volunteered before?

If so, where and when?

Why do you want to work with students?

Who are 2 references that I can call to verify your character?

Step 2: Job Description & Video Introduction

When someone submits their application, I process their background check and keep the process moving by sending them a job description and a 10-minute video to introduce them to the ministry. The video explains why student ministry is so important, what we aim to do, and how we do it.

The step is important because I want everyone, from the least involved to the most involved, to understand what we're doing and how they fit. I ask them to email me when they finish the video to schedule an observation period.

Step 3: Observation

Before I assign new volunteers a long-term role, I want them to see what they'll be doing. Most of them have an idea of what they're supposed to do from previous experiences elsewhere, but I want them to see how *we* do it.

This isn't a one-time observation. I ask them to observe for three weeks. That way, they get a feel for the level of the commitment and the other members of the team get to know them.

Step 4: Meeting

When the three weeks are over, I schedule a meeting with the potential volunteer to discuss the future. This is where I get to know the person better.

We discuss their past and where they see themselves in two years. We talk about the video and I reinforce our values and strategy. We talk about their experiences during the observation period. I answer any questions they have about serving.

Step 5: Assignment

Assuming you have a good sense that the person will do a good job, you're ready to offer them a spot on the team. Give them a starting date and celebrate them when they come aboard.

A process like this might seem overbearing, especially when you need volunteers as soon as you can get them. But I assure you, it's worth taking the time to make sure you're getting the best volunteers you can get for your students.

Today, your job is to create a process.

DAY 24

Say Thank You

Every week, your volunteers give you their most precious commodity: time. Even though you can never truly repay them for the time they invest in your ministry, saying thank you is a good start.

When you say thank you, you simultaneously give your volunteers encouragement and show them appreciation, the two things they crave the most.

When your volunteers feel encouraged and appreciated, you will see several benefits for your team:

- More positive interactions
- Higher job satisfaction
- Better performance
- Easier recruiting
- Lower turnover

In their book, *The 5 Languages of Appreciation in the Workplace,* Gary Chapman and Paul White compare encouragement and appreciation to vitamins. They say: "Taking a vitamin (or even a host of them) once really will not affect your physical system much. Their power and influence are a result of a series of small actions occurring consistently over time."[27]

Not only that, but if you've ever taken a daily multivitamin you know how easy it is to forget about it. You wake up, go through your morning routine, and head out the door. It's lunchtime before you remember that you didn't take your vitamin. Missing a day won't hurt you. But if you miss it over and over, your health will be affected negatively.

That's how it is with appreciation and encouragement. They summarize the analogy by saying, "A single act of encouragement doesn't look like it is going to change the world or make a real difference in a colleague's life. But when appreciation and encouragement are consistently communicated over a long period of time, in ways that are important to the individual – the impact can be dramatic."[28]

When you say thank you, you should be honest and specific. Don't say that you liked something when you really didn't like it. That comes across like insincere flattery and it doesn't endear anyone to you. When you honestly think someone is doing a good job, let them know about it.

Also, don't be vague. Instead of saying, "You did a great job teaching this morning," be more specific. You could say something like, "You really did a great job getting everyone's attention with that story. I could tell they were really engaged the whole time!"

You can't show too much appreciation to your volunteers. You can never encourage them enough.

There are so many ways to say thank you and help them feel special: Tell them personally, send them handwritten cards, give them gift cards, remember their birthdays, take them to lunch, praise them in front of other people. The possibilities are endless.

They're investing in your students and your ministry, so you need to make it a priority to invest in them. Help them feel encouraged and appreciated.

Today, your job is to say thank you.

DAY 25

Invite Feedback

One of the best ways to help your volunteers feel valuable and valued is to ask for their feedback. On Day 21, you evaluated them; now it's time to turn the tables. You want them to evaluate you and your programs.

Every volunteer has a unique perspective, and they all deserve a chance to share their thoughts about what's going on in the ministry.

All that you need in order to do this is a simple Google Form with a few questions on it. I send this form to each of my volunteers a few times each year.

Here are the questions I include (the scale is 1 to 5, with 5 being the best):

- *How would you rate the overall large group experience?*
- *Does the environment appear clean and ready each week?*
- *How smooth is our check-in process?*
- *How would you rate the quality of our band?*
- *How engaged are students during worship time?*

- *How much do students seem to like the games we play?*
- *How helpful are the messages?*
- *How helpful is the small group curriculum?*
- *How involved are students in the small group conversations?*
- *Do you feel like we're continuing to tweak and change things in order to get better?*
- *Do you know what's expected of you each week?*
- *Do you feel like you have the tools necessary to do your job?*

In addition to those questions, I also ask:

- *What are you most excited about in our ministry right now?*
- *Is there anything that's bugging you about our ministry right now?*
- *What is one thing that I can help you with?*
- *What is one thing that I can do better?*

If you want the responses to be honest and real, then you cannot react negatively if negative comments come your way. It's not personal; it's just their perception of how things are going. You shouldn't start pouting about it. And definitely don't argue about it. If you do, then they will stop being honest with you.

If your volunteers don't think you can handle the truth, then they'll start telling you what they think you want to hear instead of what they really think. But that won't help you get any better.

You need their honesty, so take their responses seriously and do your best to make the necessary changes. It takes thick skin to invite feedback, but it's worth it. Your volunteers will feel valuable and valued when you consider their opinions and suggestions. Plus, their comments will help you make the changes that are necessary to build a better youth ministry.

Today, your job is to invite feedback.

WEEK IN REVIEW

Day 21:

Evaluate your people. Sometimes people just need encouragement. Maybe they need training. Other times they just need a break. You need to find out which volunteers are in each category.

Day 22:

Assign roles and goals. Your volunteers need you to tell them what they're supposed to do and what translates into points on the scoreboard.

Day 23:

Create a process. You want high-performing volunteers and desperation isn't attractive to those kinds of people.

Day 24:

Say thank you. Even though you can never truly repay your volunteers for the time they invest in your ministry, saying thank you is a good start.

Day 25:

Invite feedback. Your volunteers will feel valuable and valued when you consider their opinions and suggestions.

PART 6:
Paying Attention to Your Promotion

*Reaching Out in Ways
That Attract Students*

DAY 26

Evaluate Your Promotion

Promoting your ministry is all about getting the word out: "We're here; we love students; we're having a great time; we'd love for you to join us!"

I understand that promoting your ministry might not come naturally to you. You might be afraid of coming across as pushy or arrogant. You don't want to be seen as a person who builds a bunch of hype and then doesn't live up to it.

That's understandable. I don't want to be that person either. That's why this is the last "P" that we're talking about.

We've already covered how to make your place, program, preaching, and people better. If you've done the work, then you should be seeing positive results by now. That's important.

Your promotion should only feel like hype when you claim that your ministry is the place to be and you know, deep down, that it's really not. But it's not hype when you're seeing progress, creating excitement, and having fun in your ministry.

That's not hype. **That's momentum!**

It's not pushy or arrogant to talk about the good things that are happening in your ministry. Now is the perfect time to start thinking about how to reach out in ways that attract students.

To begin with, you need to evaluate how your current promotional efforts are going. Here are a few things to consider as you evaluate:

- *What is the name of your ministry?*
- *Does each program have its own name?*
- *Are those names still relevant?*
- *What do those names communicate about who you are and what you're doing?*
- *Are there logos for your ministry and programs?*
- *Do those logos need to be updated?*
- *Does your ministry have swag for students and volunteers? (ie, shirts, stickers, pens, etc with the logo on them)*
- *Do you have a parent newsletter?*
- *Do you use a texting service?*
- *Are you building an email list?*
- *Is your church's website easy to navigate?*
- *Is the information on the website accurate?*
- *Are there typos or misspellings on printed or online documents?*
- *Would your ministry benefit from having its own website?*

- *Does your ministry have accounts on Facebook, Twitter, Instagram, YouTube, or Vimeo?*
- *If so, how often is content added to those accounts?*
- *How many followers do you have on those accounts?*
- *How many "Likes" do you get on the content you post?*
- *How are you empowering students to invite their friends?*
- *What are two creative ways to get your ministry's name and logo in front of 100 new people next month?*

When you promote your ministry, you aren't being pushy or arrogant; you're simply getting the word out. You're making a statement that you think what you're doing is worth talking about and worth showing up for.

When I first started in youth ministry, there were several times when parents would approach me a few days after an event and say that they had no idea anything was even going on. Students would complain that they didn't know what was going on. I had tried to get the word out, but apparently I hadn't done it effectively enough. Fortunately, I learned my lesson. When it comes to promotion, it's better to over communicate than under communicate.

With so many ways available to promote your ministry, there's no reason why parents and students should feel like they don't know about what's coming up. Today, your job is to evaluate your promotion.

DAY 27

Get Social

You need both students and parents to know about what's going on in your ministry. You need parents to be in the know because they provide transportation. You need students in the know because they ask their parents to drive them where they want to go.

Students won't be excited to show up at something they don't know about. Parents won't be inclined to take their kids to something they have doubts about.

One of the best ways to get the word out about your ministry or a specific event is social media. Nils Smith, author of *Social Media Guide for Ministry,* says, "When you post a video, article, church event, or any type of content on a social network, you are initiating a conversation. People can then Like, Comment, Share, or ignore your post. This interactive element completely changes the game when it comes to church communication."[29] Because social media is such a game-changer for your ministry, you want to make sure you're making the most of it.

My advice is to create accounts for your ministry on Facebook and Instagram. Twitter is a viable option too, but I haven't seen it produce half of the positive results that I've seen with Facebook for parents and Instagram for students.

Your ministry accounts should be separate from your personal accounts. The reason is simple:

You want the ministry's brand to stand on its own.

At some point in the future, you will move on to something else. When you do, you shouldn't take their pictures and memories with you. One of the things that make social media so engaging is looking back over the years and seeing how far you've come. You want those memories to remain with the ministry, not in your personal account. The ministry and the brand are bigger than you; they deserve their own accounts.

The things you post should be engaging and informative. Before you make your picture, video, or statement public, you should consider whether the intended audience would find it helpful. Is it something they would be inclined to Like, Share, or Comment on? If they wouldn't engage with the post, then either make it more engaging or don't post it.

Good things to post include:

1. What Students are Learning

- Post the Big Idea from your last message.
- Post a key statement from your last message.
- Post the Bible verse from your last message.

2. What Students are Doing

- Post a picture of last week's game winner.
- Post a picture of students serving.
- Post a picture of students singing.

3. What's Coming Up

- Post a video announcement about an upcoming event.
- Post the details that they need to know about.
- Post a question that sets up your next message.

You also want to make sure your content is up-to-date and accurate. Double-check your links to make sure they still work and take people to the correct address. Proofread your comments before and after you post them. If you notice something that needs to be changed, hit the edit button and fix it. Misspelled words and bad grammar can kill your credibility.

Your social media presence should give parents and students who have never been to your church a good sense of what's happening and what they're missing. They should see your page and think, "I'm missing out." Meanwhile, parents and students who attend your church should see your social media posts and think, "I'm glad I'm part of what's going on there."

My recommendation is to post at least one thing everyday. That level of consistency will keep your ministry on people's minds. Parents will know what's going on, and students will want to be part of what's going on.

You might be wondering how you're supposed to create all of this stuff. After all, you're not a graphic designer. Good news: you don't have to be.

I create most of my social media images with a free webbased program at Canva.com or an iPhone app called Font Candy. Both are simple to learn and easy to use.

If you want more students to sign up for your events and show up to your programs, then you have to get the word out. Social media is the fastest and most effective way to do that.

Today, your job is to get social.

DAY 28

Build Your Email List

Marketers will tell you that your email list is one your most valuable assets. That's because email gives you direct access to someone. Social media doesn't do that.

If you want to keep parents informed about what's happening in your ministry, you have to build your email list.

When you post something on Instagram, the only people who see it are those who happen to be: a) following you and b) on Instagram shortly after you posted it. It's not just Instagram. Facebook continues to change their criteria for what gets placed in someone's newsfeed and what doesn't. Don't think for a second that every parent is seeing every one of your posts. They're not.

Email is different.

Assuming you have their permission and your email doesn't sound like spam, your message will arrive in a parent's in-box just a few seconds after you press send. Even if a parent receives 100 other emails that day, your email will still get through and be seen. It's direct marketing at its best.

I didn't understand the value of an email list for youth ministry until last summer. We were getting ready for a big summer kick-off party. The event was only a few days away.

For weeks, I had posted promotional videos and images on social media. I made announcements about the event during our weekly programs. Our hope was that every student would show up and invite a friend. We were going all out for this party.

As the day of the party drew near, I tried to think of other ways to get the word out. Fortunately, I had been collecting parents' email addresses ever since I arrived at the church.

Every time a new student shows up, I have them fill out a short "About You" form. One of the lines on the form asks for a parent's email address. Every time I get a parent's email address, I add it to my list on mailchimp. com.

But I never really did anything with it.

As I thought about the most effective ways to promote the event, I decided it was time to send emails to all those parents. I gave them the key details about what we were doing, why we were doing it, where it was happening, and when they needed to show up.

It was a simple, straight-forward email that ended with a clear call to action: please bring your student and encourage them to invite a friend to come with them.

The result?

More students showed up that day than ever before!

I was inspired to email the parents on my list more often after that event. When we start a new series, I email them an overview. When we have an event coming up, I email them the details in advance. When I come across a helpful article on parenting or teenage trends, I email them a summary and a link.

When they see your name attached to an email, you want them to associate it with valuable, actionable information that will help them as a parent. Those are the kinds of emails that get opened.

Of course, you don't want to overdo it. They can always unsubscribe from your list if they feel like your emails aren't providing them with anything valuable. But most parents will appreciate the information you're providing.

I recommend sending an email to the parents on your list no more than one time each week, and no less than one time each month. Anything more than that will turn into white noise and they'll begin to tune you out. Anything less than that won't really help them feel a connection with your ministry.

Don't underestimate the power of email for promoting your ministry. Most students that I know don't use email on a regular basis, but every parent does. And those parents need to know what's going on if you expect them to bring their kids. Email is a free, easy, direct way to keep them informed.

Today, your job is to build your email list.

DAY 29

Plan Your Announcements

Making announcements during your program can be a very effective way to keep your students informed and excited about what's happening in your ministry.

I say that it *can* be because sometimes our announcements are too boring to get anyone excited, much less keep their attention. Boring announcements happen when we don't make a plan for what we want to say and how we want to say it.

If you've ever been to a wedding where someone stands up to make a toast and spends the next five minutes rambling about nine random events from the past, then you know what I'm talking about. Everyone raises their glass when that person is done talking, but no one has a clue what the point was. A little thought about what they wanted to say, and how they wanted to say it would've helped a lot.

The same thing is true when it comes to making announcements. Here are 4 guidelines for planning effective announcements:

1. Plan what you want to say.

People can only handle so much information at once. If you make five announcements, three of them will probably be forgotten by the time your program ends. Instead of filling the air with details about everything that's happening around the church, scale back and share only the two most important things that you really want everyone in the room to know about.

Don't bore them with the details. They won't remember them anyway. Besides, you can direct them to your website or give them a handout with that information. Instead, talk about what's in it for them: Why should *they* care? Why should *they* want to be there? Give them a sense that if they miss it, they're missing out.

2. Plan how you will say it.

Announcements can be creative. In fact, the more creative your announcements are, the better chance they have of being remembered. In their book, *Made to Stick,* Chip and Dan Heath point out, "Unexpected ideas are more likely to stick because surprise makes us pay attention and think...Surprise gets our attention."[30] Creative announcements get attention. They're unexpected. They're surprising. They're memorable.

Think back to the days of Show and Tell when you were a kid. Sure, you could tell your friends about the awesome ant farm you had at home in your room, but they really got excited when you actually brought it to class!

When it comes to your announcements, use props, images, and videos to talk about what's going on. You could even create walk-on characters to interrupt what's happening, deliver an important announcement, and then walk off. Think about ways to show, not just tell.

3. Plan who will say it.

You don't have to be the one to make the announcements every week. In fact, if you're doing the welcome, leading the game, and teaching the message, you probably shouldn't be the one doing the announcements too. Mix it up.

Ask a volunteer to do the announcements one week. Get a few students to help. I've enlisted everyone from the janitor to the senior pastor to come and make announcements for students.

If you're going on a retreat, you could get the speaker or the band to record a personalized video for your students. If you're going to serve somewhere, you could get a video announcement from the site coordinator saying how excited they are that your group is coming to help.

Ironically, announcements have a better chance of getting through when they come from someone other than you.

4. Plan when you will say it.

You need to decide when the best time is to make announcements in your program. It doesn't hurt to mix it up from time to time. I think the beginning is best because people are usually paying attention and it doesn't distract from the conclusion of the message.

But there are times when I'll move the announcements to the end because I want the students to immediately go out and either talk to their parents about something or sign up for it.

Also, don't forget about the most effective announcement slot: your message. When you can weave your announcement into a next action step for your message, the chance that students will hear and respond to it goes way up.

For example, in a message about serving, your next action step could be for students to sign up for a trip to a local soup kitchen or food pantry. If your message is about evangelism, then you could mention the outreach event coming up next month.

What you're doing in your ministry is important. You want your announcements to convey both information and excitement about what's coming up. That doesn't happen by accident; you have to plan for it.

Today, your job is to plan your announcements.

DAY 30

Order Swag

Swag is promotional merchandise that's used for marketing. It includes everything from t-shirts to water bottles. These everyday, ordinary items become swag when you brand them with your logo.

The first promotional products in the United States actually came from George Washington. In 1789, he created commemorative buttons for people to wear to show their support for him.

It didn't really catch on, however, until the mid 1800s when a print shop owner named Jasper Meek saw a young girl drop her schoolbooks in the middle of Main Street. That one event sparked a big idea.

Meek shared the idea with his friend, the owner of Cantwell Shoes. The idea was to imprint book bags with a simple advertising message: "Buy Cantwell Shoes." The bags were created and given to every child who came into the store. When those children walked to and from school, the Cantwell brand was seen all over town. The idea proved so successful that Meek created the Tuscarora Advertising Company, and went on to print advertisements on anything that could be put through a printing press: calendars, hats, playing cards, and even aprons.

Imagine what might happen at your church if every one of your students wore a shirt with your ministry's logo on it to school on Wednesday. It would definitely spark some conversations. By the end of the day, other students would be saying, "I've seen that logo before. What's happening there?"

When it comes to swag, you want to choose items that your students will *want* to use or wear in public. If they wouldn't use it, then don't waste your money on it. The point is to create brand awareness for your ministry.

The marketing team at Apple takes brand awareness seriously. Whenever someone buys an Apple product, they also get Apple stickers in the box.

Why does Apple give those stickers away?

The reason is simple: free advertising. People put those stickers on their cars, guitar cases, refrigerators, and anywhere else that has a flat, visible surface for all to see. Those simple, inexpensive stickers create enormous brand awareness for Apple.

Those stickers also create social proof. They prove that someone has purchased an Apple product. That proof makes other people more inclined to purchase them too. In his book, *Contagious,* Jonah Berger explains why this happens. He says, "We assume that if other people are doing something, it must be a good idea. They probably know something we don't."[31]

When you order t-shirts or stickers or pens or bags or water bottles with your logo on them for your students, you aren't just giving your students a little token of appreciation. You're mobilizing them to spread your brand on their campuses. They become walking billboards for your ministry.

When their friends, classmates, and teammates see their swag, they'll be intrigued. They'll ask about it. They'll want it too (assuming it's good). And then your students will simply say, "Come to my church. You can get one there. Actually, we've got this cool thing that we're doing next Wednesday night. Why don't you come with me?" All of the attempts to create brand awareness and social proof pay off in that moment because that personal invitation is the best promotion your ministry will ever get.

Today, your job is to order swag.

WEEK IN REVIEW

Day 26:

Evaluate your promotion. Now is the perfect time to start thinking about how to reach out in ways that attract students.

Day 27:

Get social. Because social media is such a game-changer for your ministry, you want to make sure you're making the most of it.

Day 28:

Build your email list. Don't underestimate the power of email for promoting your ministry. Email is a free, easy, direct way to keep them informed.

Day 29:

Plan your announcements. Making announcements during your program is an effective way to keep your students informed and excited about what's happening in your ministry.

Day 30:

Order swag. Swag mobilizes your students to spread your brand on their campuses. They become walking billboards for your ministry.

CONCLUSION

Better Before Bigger...

Two decades ago, Chick-fil-A's executive team gathered to discuss a threat to their business. A new restaurant was on the scene. It was another chicken restaurant with big goals and expansion plans.

The executives nervously assembled to talk about what to do next. The conversation quickly became focused on growing bigger and faster. They wanted to outdo their new competitor, Boston Market.

Truett Cathy, the founder of Chick-fil-A, was in the meeting. Truett, a mild mannered man by all accounts, started pounding his fist on the table to get everyone's attention. He said, "Gentlemen, I am sick and tired of hearing you talk about us getting bigger. What we need to be talking about is getting better. If we get better, our customers will demand that we get bigger."

Truett's recipe was right. The company continued working to get better – better food options, better personnel, better store designs – and as a result, they've grown bigger.

The same principle applies to your youth ministry:

When your ministry gets better, it will grow bigger.

The staff covenant at North Point has 6 commitments. Each of those commitments has a corresponding question that makes it personal for each staff member. Number two on that list is, "Make It Better: What am I doing personally to help us improve organizationally?" I recommend printing that question and hanging it in your office to be a daily reminder.

All of us want our ministries to grow bigger. We all want to reach more students. We all want to baptize more students. We all want to help more students grow in their faith. The key to getting bigger is to get better.

This book has given you 30 ways to build a better youth ministry in 30 days. I hope you've done the work and seen great results.

This is just the start. Keep evaluating. Keep dreaming. Keep praying. Keep trying new things. Keep improving. Keep getting better. It's only a matter of time until your ministry starts getting bigger!

DID YOU ENJOY THIS BOOK?

I want to thank you for purchasing and reading this book. I really hope you got a lot out of it.

Can I ask you to do me a quick favor?

If you enjoyed this book, I would really appreciate a positive review on Amazon. I love getting feedback, and reviews really do make a difference.

Scan to go directly to my Author Page on Amazon. Click on the book and write your review. I read all of my reviews and would really appreciate your thoughts. You can also connect with me on Twitter at @betteryouthmin

Thank you!

DOWNLOAD YOUR
FREE RESOURCES

To say thank you for your purchase, I'd like to send you a free bonus package. This includes a cheat sheet of the big ideas covered in this book, along with an mp3 coaching lesson on leading volunteers and a 2-week message series you can use with your students.

Download your free bonus package today at:

www.betteryouthministry.com/30 days

LOOKING FOR ONE ON ONE COACHING?

I can help your youth ministry gain momentum and get results.

Here are some of the ways I can help:

Resources

From administrative templates to games to message series, I can connect you with tools that will immediately take your ministry to the next level.

Strategy

Some things create more impact and more results than others. I can help you discover what's holding you back and how to move forward.

Volunteer Training

Your ministry will only be as good as the leaders around you. I can help you recruit, train, and inspire your volunteers.

Personal Development

You are a combination of the books you read, the people

you spend time with, and the podcasts you listen to. I can point you in the right direction.

Communication

How you say what you say is important. I can help you craft compelling messages that get students to respond.

Learn more at:

www.betteryouthministry.com/coaching

ABOUT THE AUTHOR

Trevor Hamaker helps youth pastors do ministry better. He has over a decade of youth ministry experience, along with degrees in business management, organizational leadership, and religious education. Find out more at betteryouthministry.com.

MORE BOOKS BY
TREVOR HAMAKER

People Skills for Youth Pastors: 33 Ways to Meet More People and Make a Bigger Difference in Youth Ministry

Your First 90 Days in a New Youth Ministry: A Simple Plan for Starting Right

Varsity Faith: A Thoughtful, Humble, Intentional, and Hopeful Option for Christian Students

END NOTES

1. James C. Collins and Jerry I. Porras, *Built to Last: Successful Habits of Visionary Companies* (New York, NY: HarperBusiness, 1997), 10.

2. Carol Dweck, *Mindset: The New Psychology of Success* (New York, NY: Ballantine Books, 2006), 7.

3. Matt Slater, "Olympics Cycling: Marginal Gains Underpin Team GB Dominance," BBC. Online: http:// www.bbc.com/sport/olympics/19174302 (accessed 2 December 2015).

4. *Built to Last,* 232.

5. http://www.daveramsey.com/blog/what-is-a-bhagand-why-do-you-need-one/ (accessed 3 December 2015).

6. Brian Tracy, *Goals! How to Get Everything You Want – Fast Than You Ever Thought Possible* (San Francisco, CA: Berrett-Koehler, 2003), 7.

7. Will Mancini, "The 11 Minute Difference: 7 Checkpoints to a Great Guest Experience at Your Church." Online: http://www.willmancini. com/2010/09/the-11-minute-difference-7checkpoints-to-a-great-guest-experience-at-yourchurch.html (accessed 4 December 2015).

8. Nelson Searcy, "How to Make a Great FirstTime Guest Impression." Online: https://www. churchleaderinsights.com/index.php/free-stuff/ how-to-make-a-great-first-time-guest-impression (accessed 4 December 2015).

9. Mark Waltz, *First Impressions: Creating Wow Experiences in Your Church* (Loveland, CO: Group Publishing, 2004), 41.

10. Malcolm Gladwell, *The Tipping Point: How Little Things Can Make a Big Difference* (New York, NY: Back Bay Books, 2002), 141.

11. Andy Stanley, *Deep and Wide: Creating Churches Unchurched People Love to Attend* (Grand Rapids, MI: Zondervan, 2012), 168.

12. Kurt Johnston, *99 Thoughts about Junior High Ministry: Tips, Tricks, and Tidbits for Working with Young Teenagers* (Loveland, CO: Group Publishing, 2012), 3.

13. Thom Rainer, *Surprising Insights from the Unchurched and Proven Ways to Reach Them* (Grand Rapids, MI: Zondervan, 2001), 56.

14. http://panopto.com/blog/the-single-greatestsecret-to-delivering-a-perfect-presentation-recordyourself-practicing/ (accessed 20 January 2016).

15. Charles Spurgeon, *Lectures to My Students* (Grand Rapids, MI: Zondervan, 1956), 84-85.

16. Rick Warren, *The Purpose-Driven Church* (Grand Rapids, MI: Zondervan, 1995), 165.

17. David Buttrick, *Homiletic: Moves and Structures* (Philadelphia, PA: Fortress Press, 1987), 28.

18. Andy Stanley and Lane Jones, *Communicating for a Change* (Sisters, OR: Multnomah, 2006), 125.

19. Carmine Gallo, *The Presentation Secrets of Steve Jobs: How to Be Insanely Great in Front of Any Audience* (New York, NY: McGraw Hill, 2010), 40.

20. Fred Craddock, *As One Without Authority*, 4th edition (St. Louis, MO: Chalice Press, 2001), 14.

21. Michael Lipka, "A Closer Look at America's Rapidly Growing Religious 'Nones,' *Pew Research.* Online: http://www.pewresearch.org/facttank/2015/05/13/a-closer-look-at-americas-rapidlygrowing-religious-nones/ (accessed 22 January 2016).

22. Cited in Ralph Lewis and Greg Lewis, *Inductive Preaching: Helping People Listen* (Westchester, IL: Crossway Books, 1983), 24.

23. Doug Fields and Duffy Robbins, *Speaking to Teenagers: How to Think About, Create, and Deliver Effective Messages* (Grand Rapids, MI: Zondervan, 2007), 49.

24. Jim Collins, *Good to Great: Why Some Companies Make the Leap...and Others Don't* (New York, NY: HarperCollins, 2001), 41.

25. Andy Stanley, Reggie Joiner, and Lane Jones, *7 Practices of Effective Ministry* (Sisters, OR: Multnomah, 2004), 72.

26. *Ibid.,* 72.

27. Gary D. Chapman and Paul E. White, *The 5 Languages of Appreciation in the Workplace: Empowering Organizations by Encouraging People* (Chicago, IL: Northfield Publishing, 2011), 231.

28. *Ibid.*, 232.

29. Nils Smith, *Social Media Guide for Ministry* (Loveland, CO: Group Publishing, 2013), 7.

30. Chip Heath and Dan Heath, *Made to Stick: Why Some Ideas Survive and Others Die* (New York, NY: Random House, 2007), 68.

31. Jonah Berger, *Contagious: Why Things Catch On* (New York, NY: Simon & Schuster 2013), 128.

Notes

64979590R00090

Made in the USA
Lexington, KY
26 June 2017